My Big Book of ABC 123

Letters **3**

Numbers **27**

Words **49**

Animals **73**

Miles Kelly

First published in 2015 by Miles Kelly Publishing Ltd
Harding's Barn, Bardfield End Green, Thaxted, Essex, CM6 3PX, UK

Copyright © Miles Kelly Publishing Ltd 2015

2 4 6 8 10 9 7 5 3 1

Publishing Director Belinda Gallagher
Creative Director Jo Cowan
Editorial Director Rosie Neave
Senior Editor Sarah Parkin
Senior Designer Rob Hale
Production Elizabeth Collins, Caroline Kelly
Reprographics Stephan Davis, Jennifer Cozens, Thom Allaway
Consultant Susan Purcell

ISBN 978-1-78209-821-8

Printed in China

British Library Cataloguing-in-Publication Data
A catalogue record for this book is available from the British Library

ACKNOWLEDGEMENTS
The publishers would like to thank the following artists who have contributed to this book:
Letters: Richard Watson, Numbers: Michael Garton, Words: Heather Heyworth, Animals: Nik Afia

Made with paper from a sustainable forest

www.mileskelly.net
info@mileskelly.net

Letters

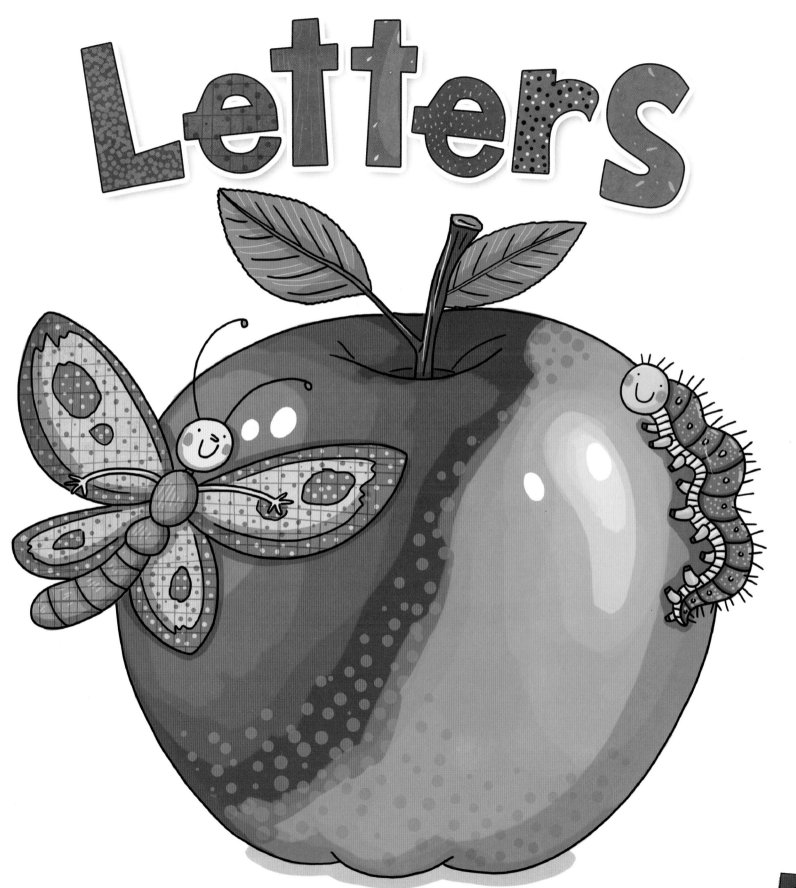

3

Aa

apple

ant

astronaut

ambulance

anchor

a b c d e f g h i j k l m n

Bb

What colour is the balloon?

balloon

boy

bus

bicycle

ball

book

butterfly

o p q r s t u v w x y z

5

C c

car

clock

castle

How many candles are on the cake?

caterpillar

cat

cake

cow

a b c d e f g h i j k l m n

Dd

dragon

dog

dolphin

dinosaur

digger

Ee

How many ears does the elephant have?

elephant

egg

elf

envelope

a b c d e f g h i j k l m n

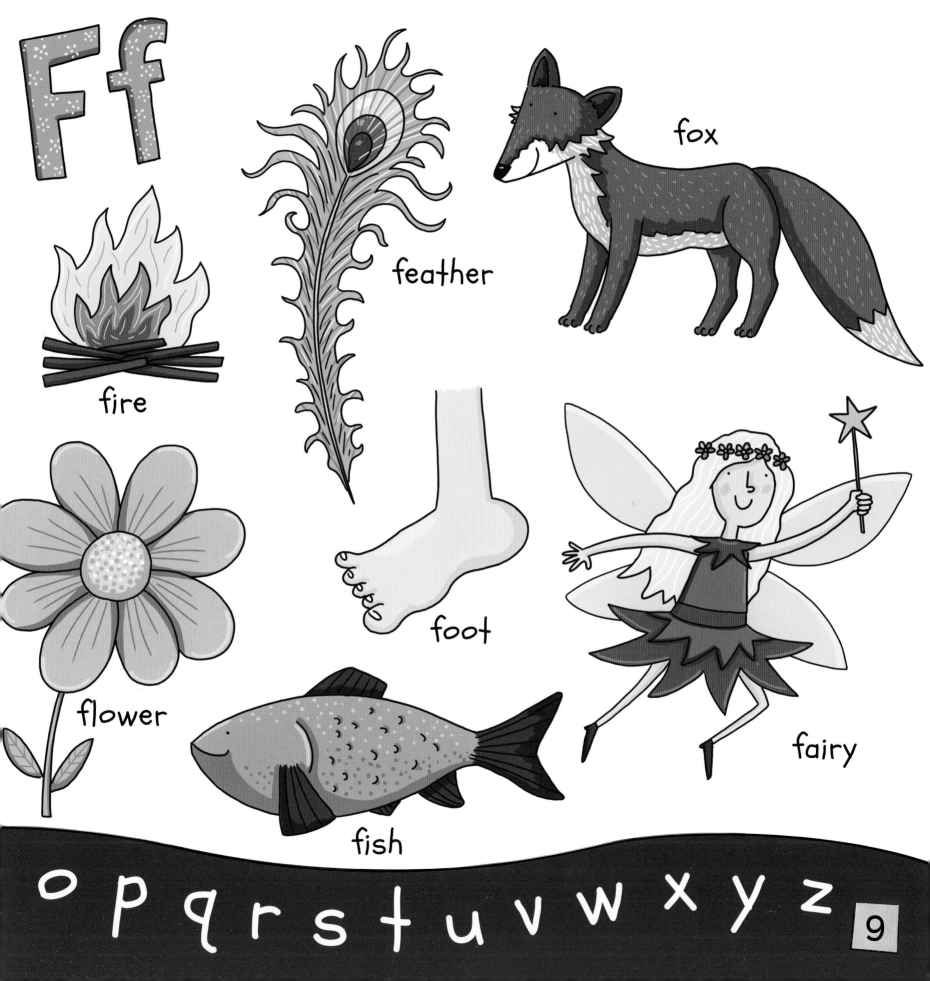

Ff

fox

feather

fire

flower

foot

fairy

fish

Gg

goose

grapes

goat

What colour are the gloves?

girl

gloves

ghost

a b c d e f g h i j k l m n

Hh

helicopter

hen

hand

horse

hat

hair

head

Ii

igloo

iguana

invitation

Jj

jigsaw

juice

jug

jewels

a b c d e f g h i j k l m n

Kk

kite

key

kitten

king

How many bows
are on the kite?

o p q r s t u v w x y z

13

Ll

ladybird

lemon

leaf

How many spots are on the ladybird?

lamb

lion

a b c d e f g h i j k l m n

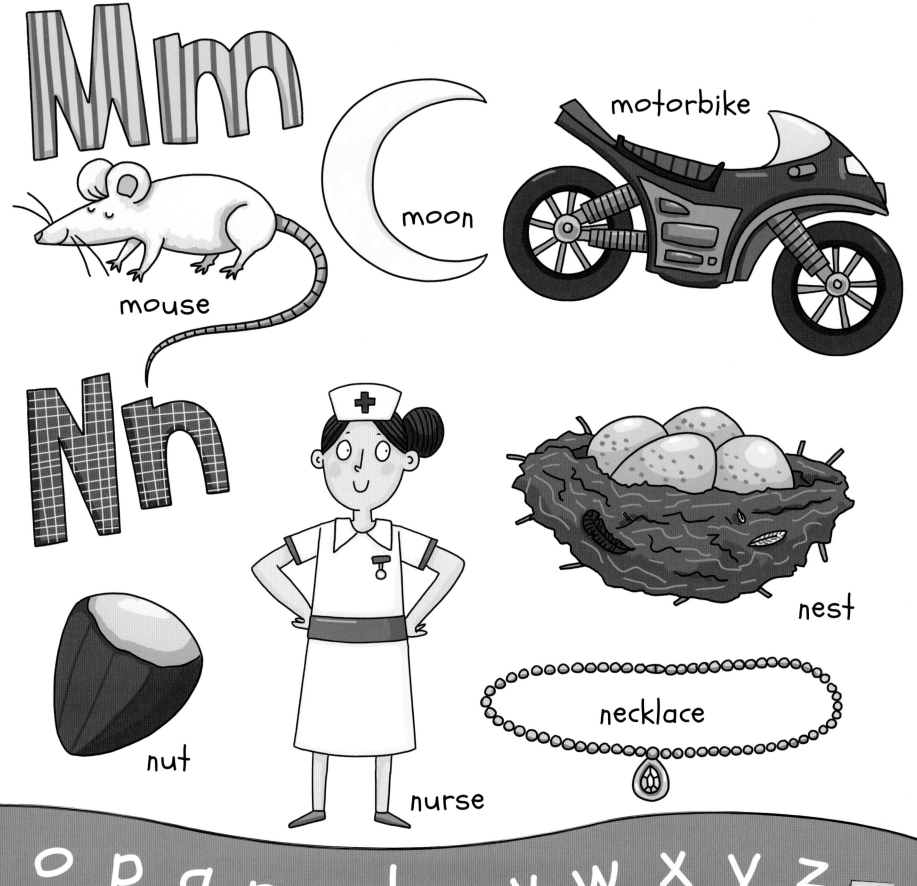

Mm

mouse

moon

motorbike

Nn

nut

nurse

nest

necklace

Oo

ostrich

octopus

orange

Pp

princess

pizza

present

a b c d e f g h i j k l m n

pirate

penguin

puppy

What colour
is the princess's
dress?

pencil

paper

paint

paintbrush

Qq

quilt

question mark

queen

Rr

rabbit

rain

rainbow

a b c d e f g h i j k l m n

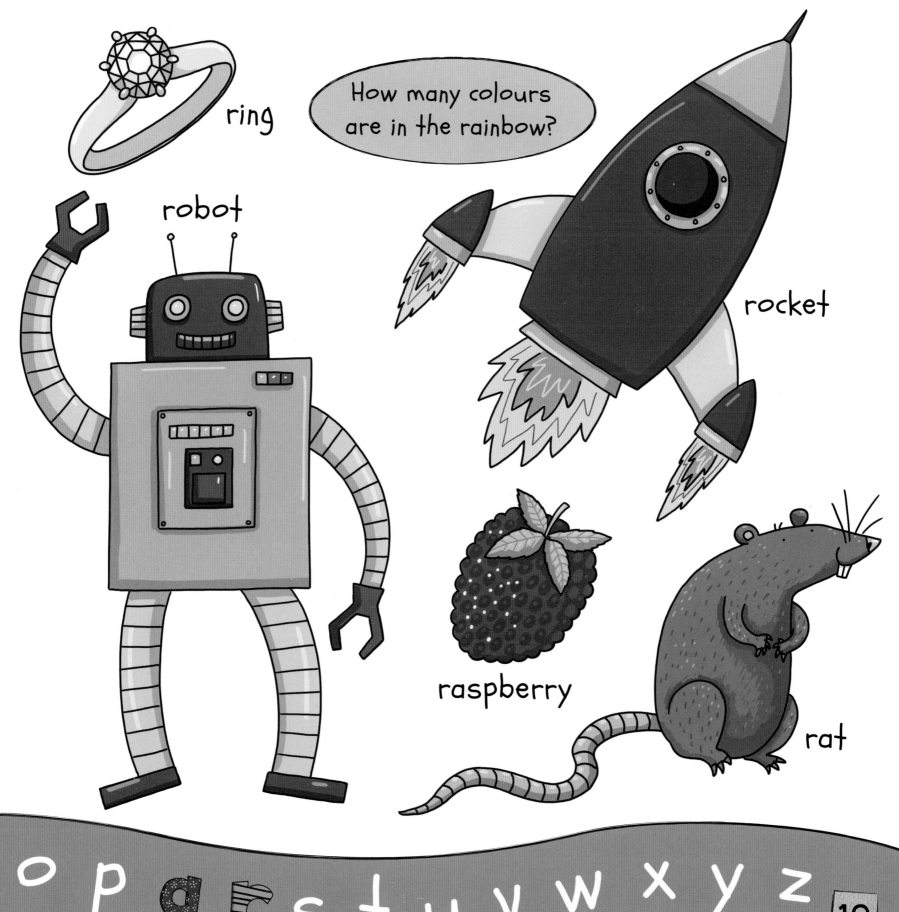

ring

How many colours are in the rainbow?

robot

rocket

raspberry

rat

o p q r s t u v w x y z

19

Ss

sandwich

sun

snake

What pattern is on the socks?

slippers

sausage

socks

seahorse

a b c d e f g h i j k l m n

Tt

train

tomato

teddy

tractor

tree

tiger

toothpaste

toothbrush

o p q r s t u v w x y z

21

U u

up

upstairs

umbrella

V v

vase

volcano

van

a b c d e f g h i j k l m n

W w

watch

wheel

web

wand

What colour is the wizard's beard?

whistle

whale

wizard

o p q r s t u v w x y z

23

X x

x-ray

xylophone

What colour is the yo-yo?

Y y

yoghurt

yo-yo

yacht

a b c d e f g h i j k l m n

Zz

zip

zigzag

zebra

zero

Can you find?

Look back on pages 4-25 to see if you can find the following things.

butterfly

fox

grapes

leaf

motorbike

pizza

Sun

Umbrella

Numbers

1 comfy bed
one

What colour is the pillow?

Can you find? **1** lamp **1** clock

2 two teddy bears

1 ball

2 books

2 pictures

3 racing go-karts

three

Can you find? **3** balloons **1** helter-skelter

4 carousel horses

four

What colour is the tasty candy floss?

3 basketballs   4 tents   4 flags

31

5 five party hats

Can you find? 5 candles 5 drinks

6 big balloons

six

How many blue balloons can you find?

6 cupcakes   4 presents   6 hot dogs

7 rubber rings

seven

How many pink swimming hats can you see?

34 Can you find? 1 lifeguard 7 floats

8 eight

happy swimmers

4 flip flops **5** towels **8** armbands

9 exercise books

nine

What shape is the clock on the wall?

Everyone needs a paintbrush!

WOOF!

Can you find?

 1 teacher

 10 paintbrushes

10 ten excited children

MEOW!

a

9 pencils

6 lunchboxes

WOOF!

4 posters

11 woolly sheep
eleven

What is the cat chasing?

38 Can you find? 2 cats 1 tractor

12 clucking chickens

twelve

4 mice   5 haystacks   3 cows

14 fluttery butterflies

fourteen

5 lily pads 6 flowers 4 bees

15 yellow bananas

fifteen

Can you find? 9 apples 5 peppers

16

sixteen

crunchy carrots

What colour are the juicy apples?

2 trolleys

8 cherries

3 pineapples

17 tweeting birds

seventeen

We could be flying or looking for food!

Can you find? 2 kites 6 wheels

18 pretty flowers

eighteen

How many white flowers can you see?

4 clouds

3 trees

1 dog

19 waving flags

nineteen

How many red flags can you find?

Can you find? **1** ice cream **2** children

20 pink seashells

twenty

3 starfish

4 gulls

5 crabs

47

Can you find?

Look back on pages 28-47 to see if you can find the following things.

plane

cake

ball

clock

horse

basket

swings

bucket

Words

49

At home

bedroom

curtains

bed

drawers

wardrobe

fridge

kitchen

cooker

cupboards

What colour are the curtains in the bedroom?

50

bathroom

toilet

sink

bath

television

window

door

sofa

lounge

How many of these objects have you got in your home?

In the home

telephone

lamp

clock

cushion

chair

book

table

Can you name the animal on the lamp?

Toys

teddy

car

jigsaw

train

dinosaur

blocks

doll

What are your favourite toys to play with?

In the garden

shed

fence

strawberries

carrots

bee

caterpillar

leaf

grass

dog

How many carrots are growing in the garden?

washing

bird

bush

ball

tree

butterfly

flowers

cat

What other things might be in a garden?

In the family

Grandad

Grandma

Daddy

Mummy

baby

sister

brother

How many people are there in this family?

My body

head

hair

ear

face

nose

eye

mouth

teeth

arm

tummy

hand

fingers

knee

leg

foot

toes

Can you point to these parts of your body?

57

On the street

park

bus

house

flats

bus stop

car

zebra crossing

motorbike

road

What colour is the car?

roof

shop

bicycle

pavement

pram

Which shops do you like best?

Things that go

aeroplane

hot-air balloon

train

truck

tractor

60

How many of these vehicles can fly?

ambulance

helicopter

digger

ferry

fire engine

yacht

Which of these vehicles have you seen?

At the park

sky

kite

boat

path

pond

bicycle

ducks

picnic

ice cream

blanket

How many ducks can you see?

cloud

squirrel

bench

slide

swings

What do you like to do at the park?

63

Picnic food

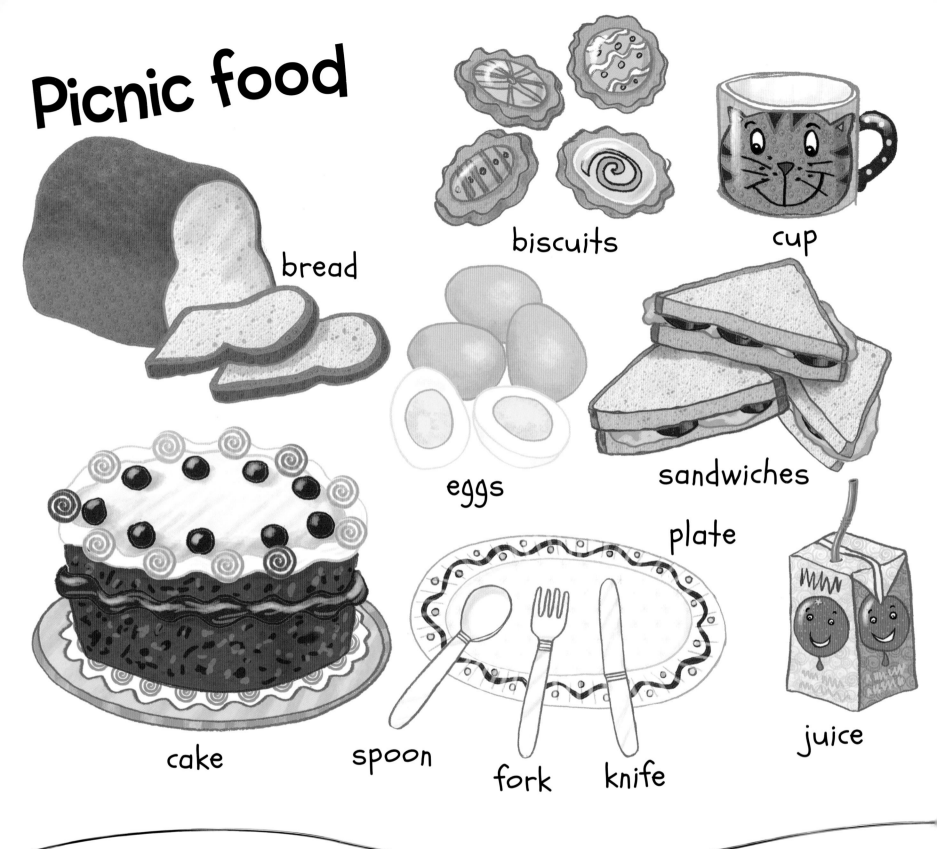

bread

biscuits

cup

eggs

sandwiches

plate

cake

spoon

fork

knife

juice

How many different foods are in the salad?

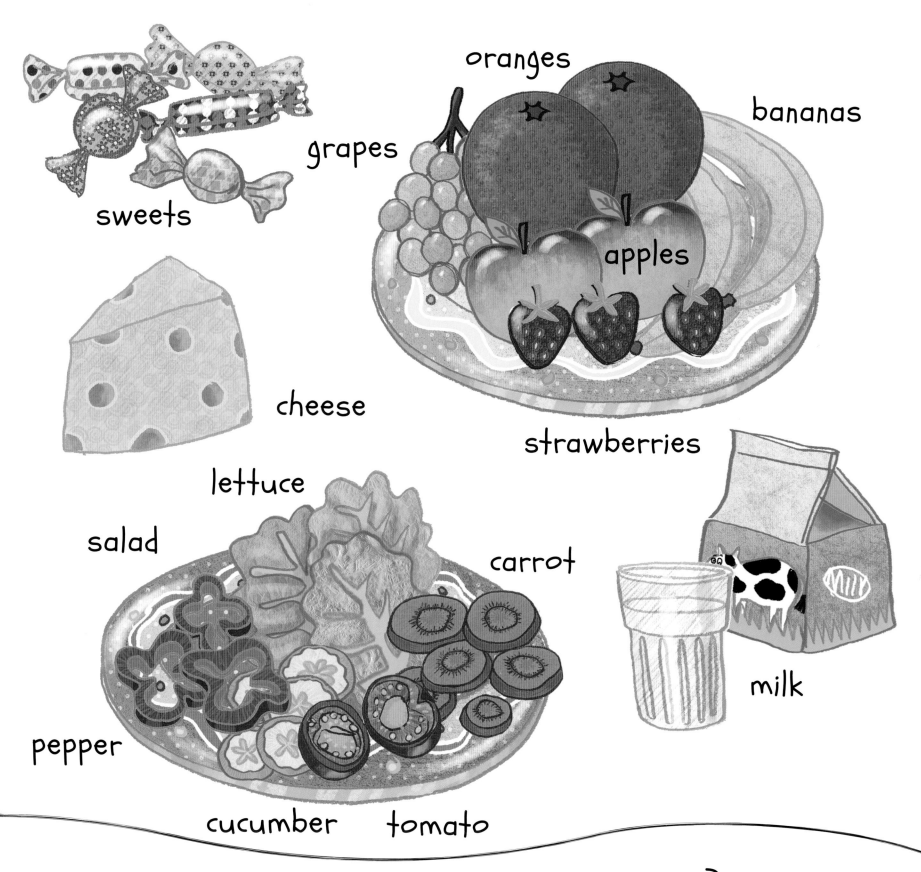

sweets

grapes

oranges

bananas

apples

cheese

strawberries

lettuce

salad

carrot

milk

pepper

cucumber   tomato

What food do you like to eat on a picnic?

On the beach

gull

boat

waves

spade

sandcastle

boy

bucket

shell

66

How many shells can you find?

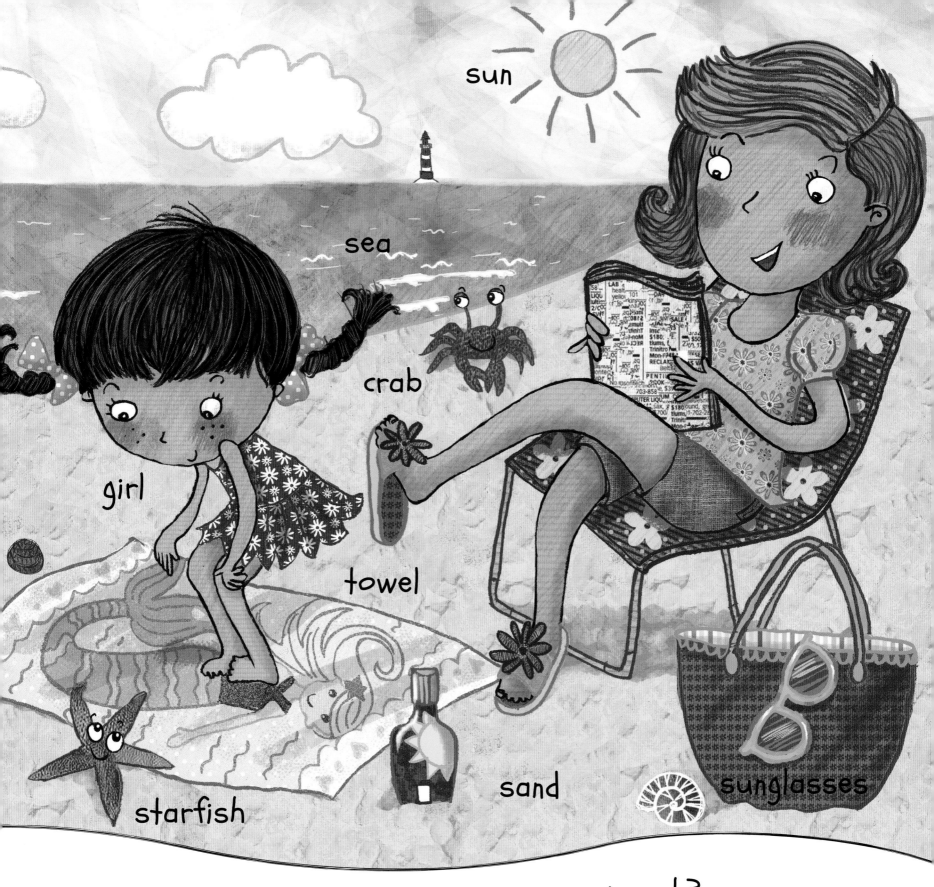

sun

sea

crab

girl

towel

starfish

sand

sunglasses

What do you like doing on the beach?

Clothes

shorts

jumper

dress

t-shirt

socks

scarf

skirt

gloves

vest

pants

coat

shoes

trousers

Which of these clothes do you wear when it is cold?

Colours

black

green

yellow

blue

red

pink

brown

purple

orange

white

What colour clothes are you wearing?

69

Shapes

triangle

square

circle

rectangle

star

oval

diamond

heart

What shape is an egg?

Numbers

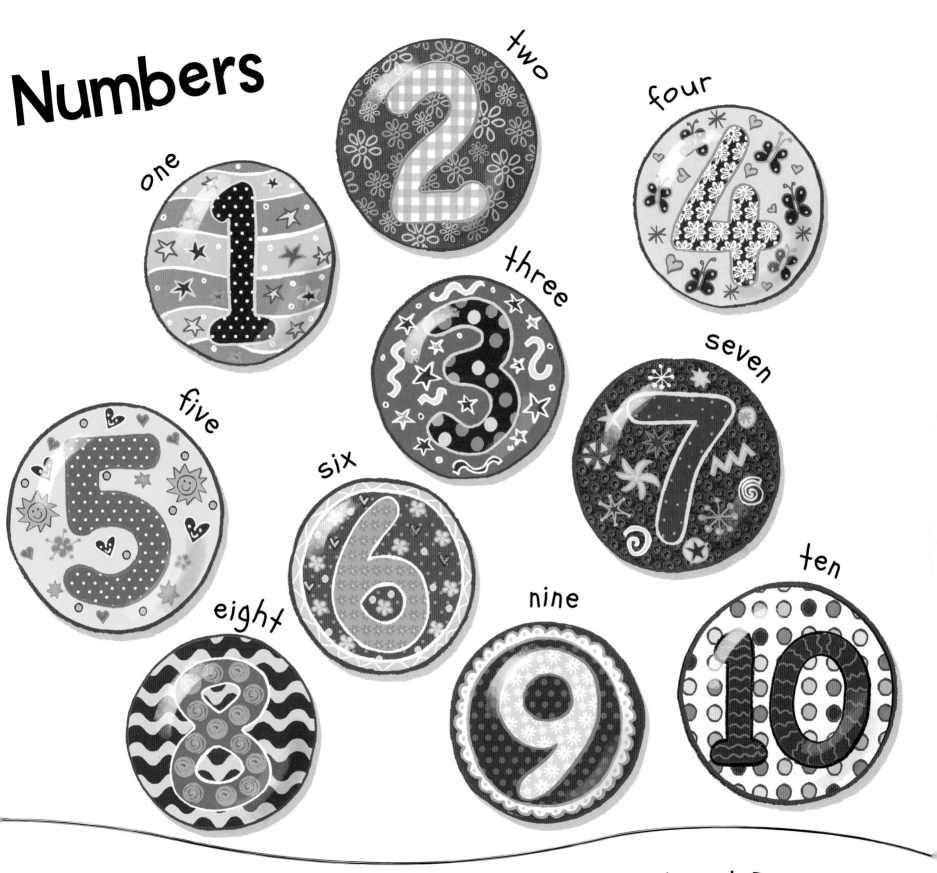

one
two
three
four
five
six
seven
eight
nine
ten

Can you count all the way from one to twenty?

Can you find?

Look back on pages 50–71 to see if you can find the following things.

clock

teddy

dinosaur

hot-air balloon

yacht

72 sandwiches

sweets

t-shirt

73

Forests and woods

raccoon

Eagles have sharp beaks and claws.

squirrel

wolf

eagle

deer

fox

Which black-and-white animal is eating bamboo?

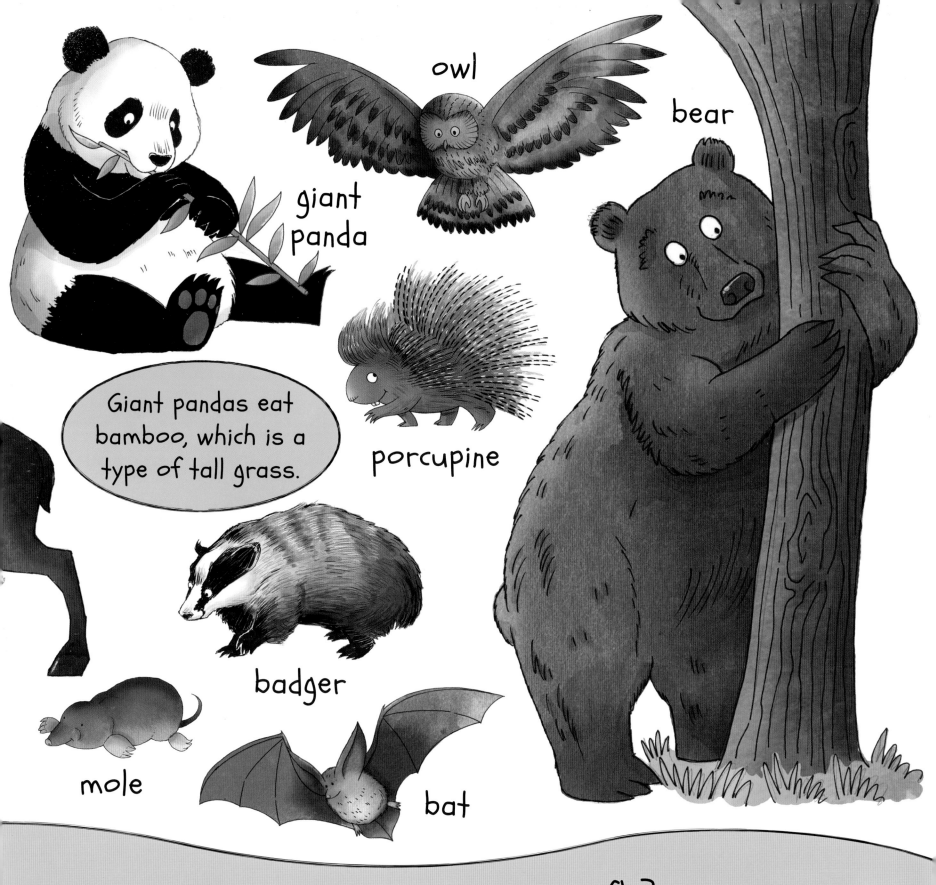

owl

bear

giant
panda

Giant pandas eat
bamboo, which is a
type of tall grass.

porcupine

badger

mole

bat

Which of these animals can fly?

Rivers and lakes

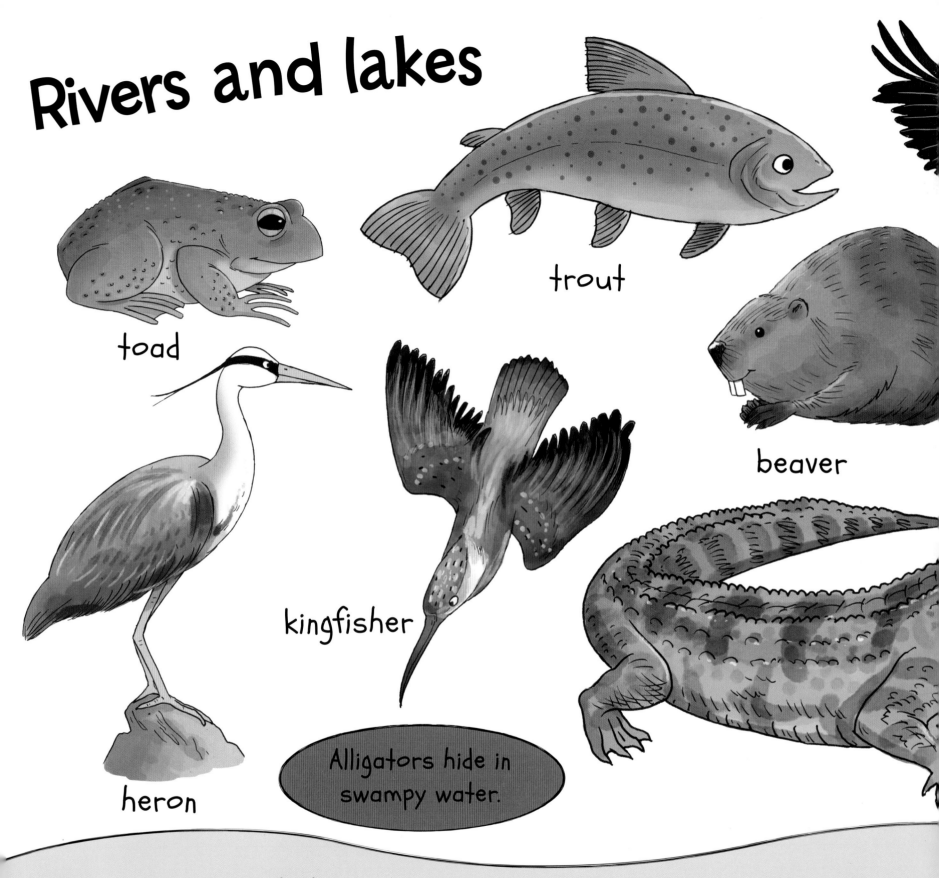

trout

toad

beaver

heron

kingfisher

Alligators hide in swampy water.

Which animal has pink feathers?

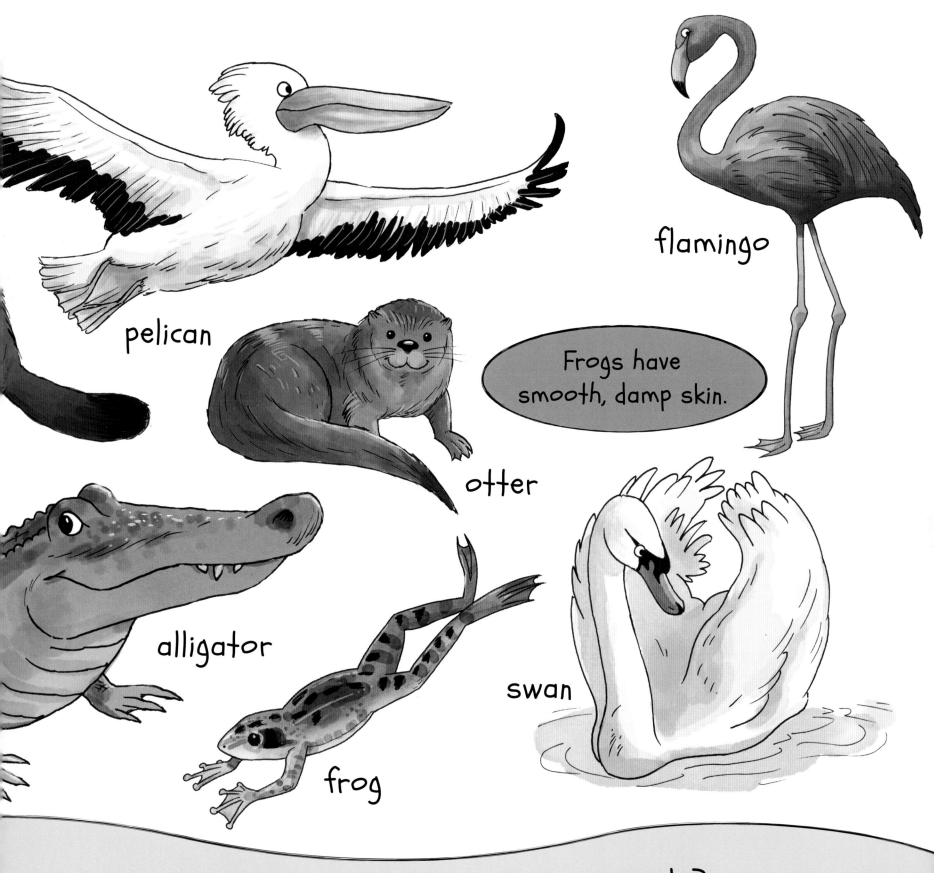

pelican

flamingo

otter

Frogs have smooth, damp skin.

alligator

swan

frog

How many of these animals are birds?

In the jungle

All snakes are meat eaters.

toucan

emerald tree boa

butterfly

orang-utan

gorilla

iguana

lemur

What kind of animal is a tarantula?

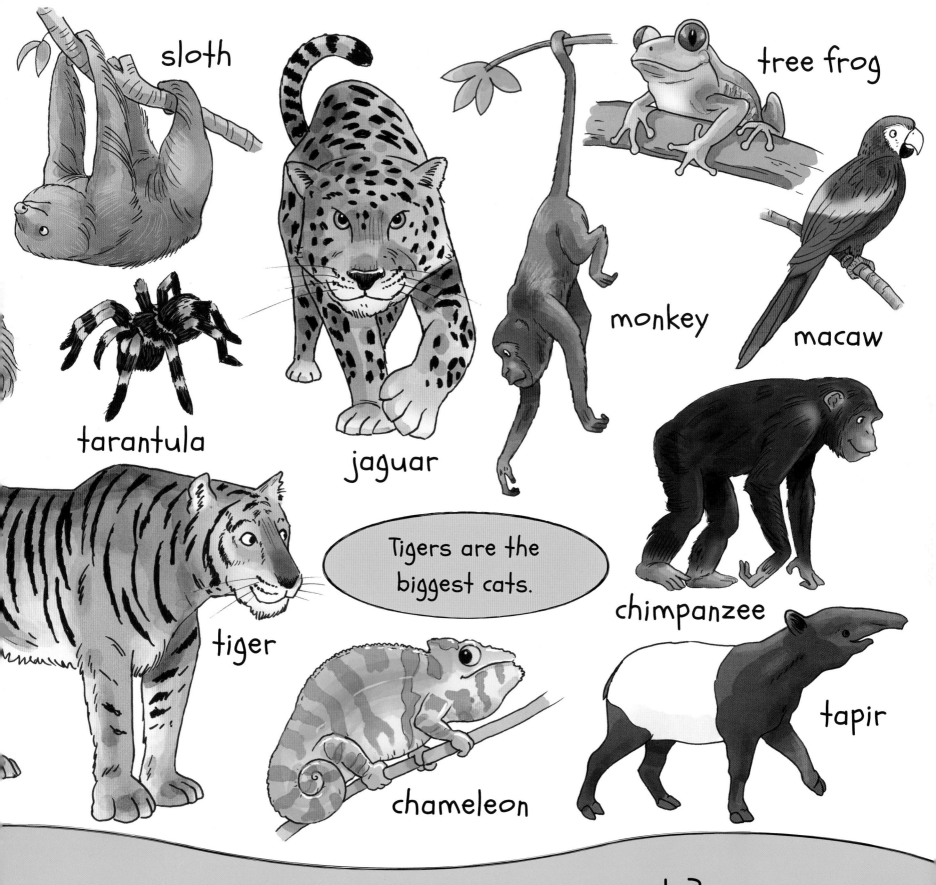

sloth

tree frog

jaguar

monkey

macaw

tarantula

tiger

Tigers are the biggest cats.

chimpanzee

chameleon

tapir

How many of these animals are cats?

On the seashore

scallop

mussel

gull

Sea anemones catch food with their tentacles.

crab

starfish

sea anemone

Which animal has a body shaped like a star?

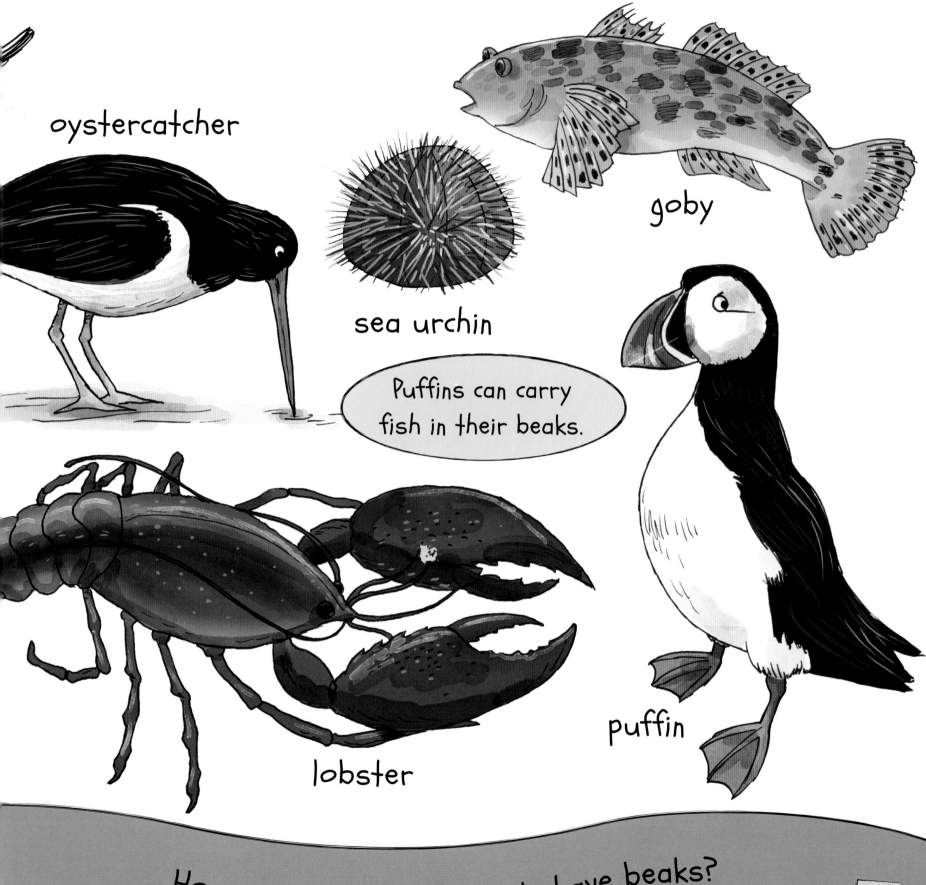

oystercatcher

sea urchin

goby

Puffins can carry fish in their beaks.

lobster

puffin

How many of these animals have beaks?

81

Seas and oceans

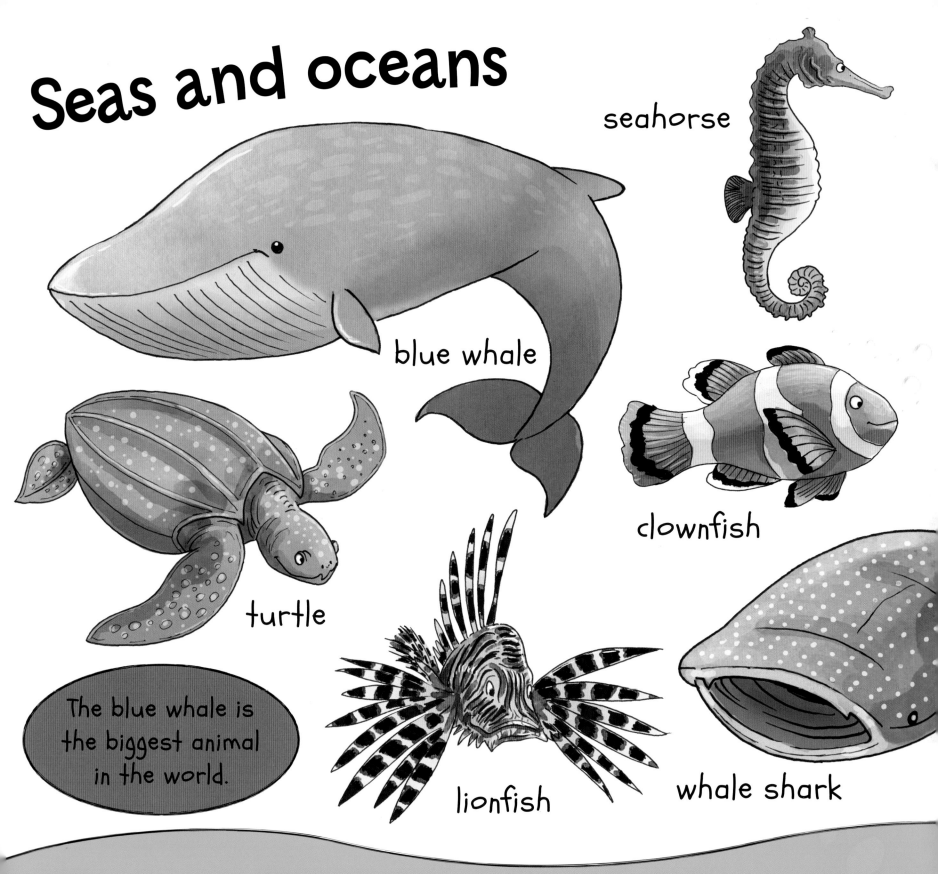

seahorse

blue whale

clownfish

turtle

The blue whale is the biggest animal in the world.

lionfish

whale shark

Which fish looks like a spiky ball?

octopus

dolphin

pufferfish

Pufferfish swallow water to make them swell up.

ray

jellyfish

great white shark

Which of these animals are sharks?

83

In the desert

fennec fox

camel

scorpion

Scorpions can survive without water for months.

lizard

kangaroo rat

sidewinder snake

Which animal has two large humps on its back?

Australian animals

Kangaroos jump using their back legs.

dingo

kangaroo

kookaburra

emu

koala

cassowary

Which bird has a large, horny crest on its head?

85

African animals

vulture

leopard

hyena

Elephants are the biggest land animals.

elephant

wildebeest

lion

rhinoceros

crocodile

Which animal has a long trunk?

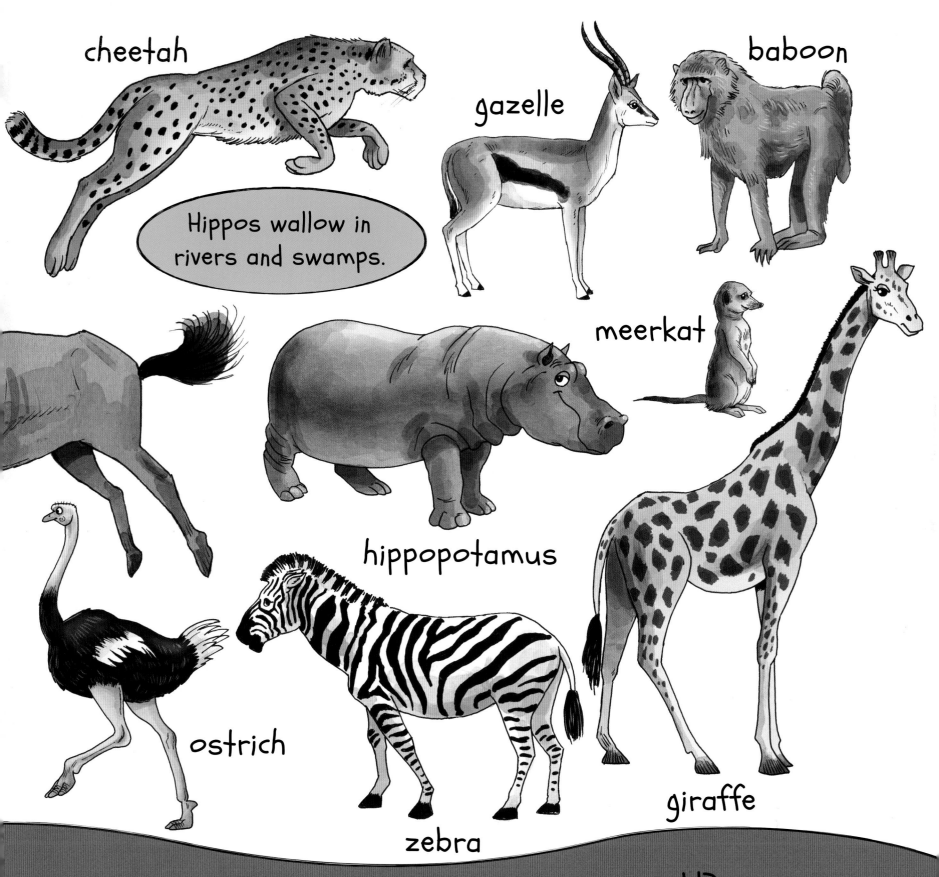

cheetah

gazelle

baboon

Hippos wallow in rivers and swamps.

meerkat

hippopotamus

ostrich

zebra

giraffe

What is the tallest animal in the world?

In the Arctic

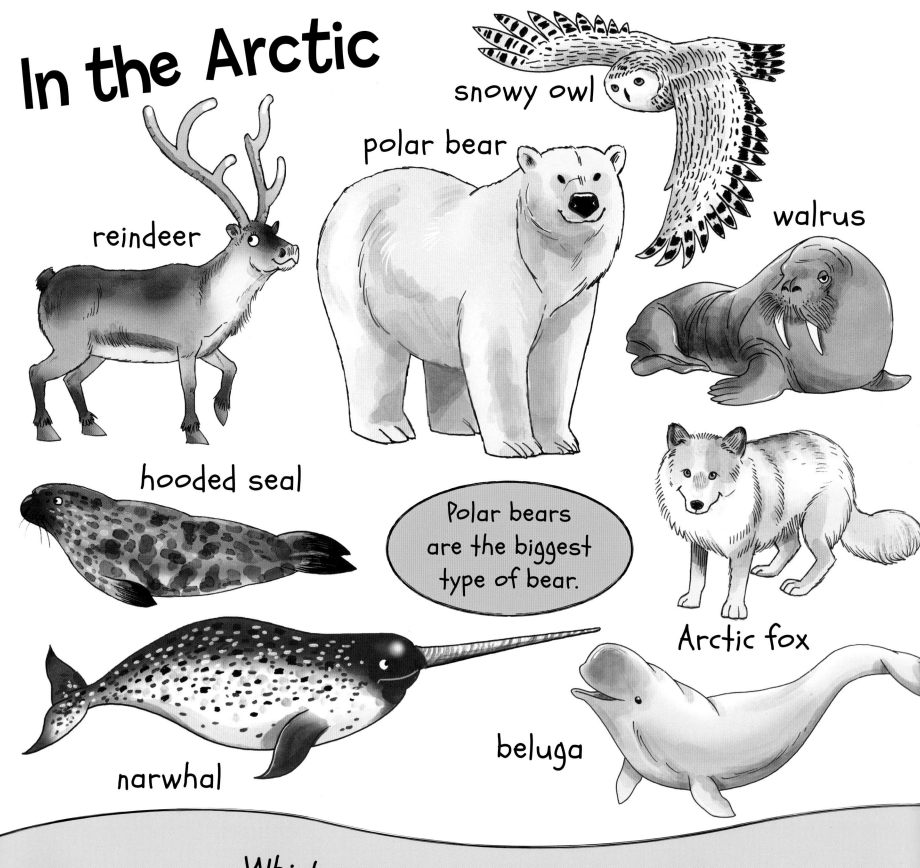

snowy owl

polar bear

walrus

reindeer

hooded seal

Polar bears are the biggest type of bear.

Arctic fox

narwhal

beluga

Which animal has two large tusks?

In the Antarctic

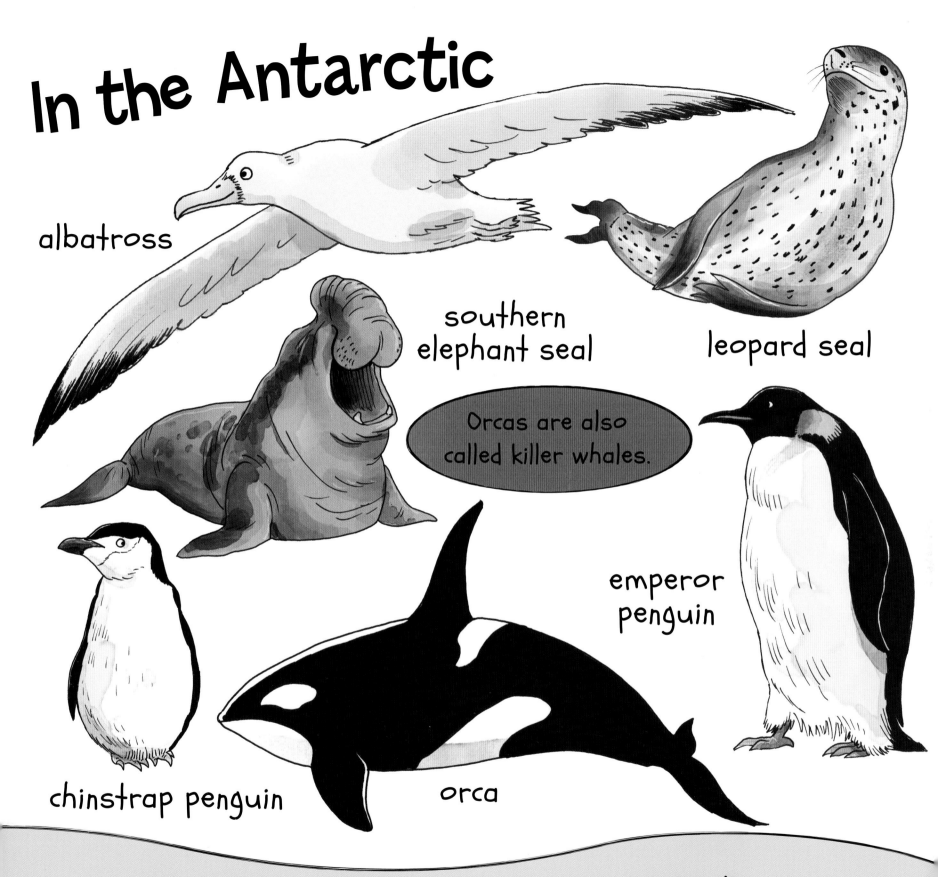

albatross

southern elephant seal

leopard seal

Orcas are also called killer whales.

emperor penguin

chinstrap penguin

orca

Which penguin is the biggest swimming bird?

On the farm

sheep

goose

pig

Sheep grow thick coats to keep them warm in winter.

cow

chicken

What is the name for a group of cows?

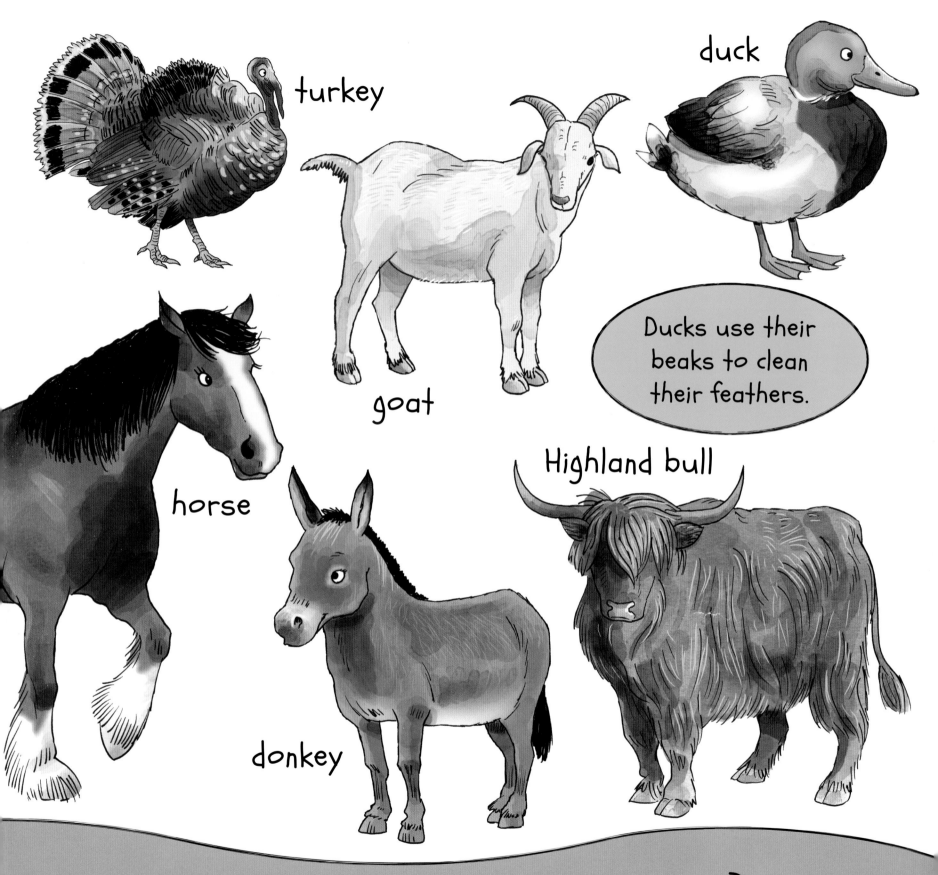

turkey

duck

goat

Ducks use their beaks to clean their feathers.

horse

Highland bull

donkey

How many of these animals have you seen?

Minibeasts

moth

dragonfly

Dragonflies catch food with their legs.

grasshopper

stag beetle

bee

ant

Which minibeast is red with black spots?

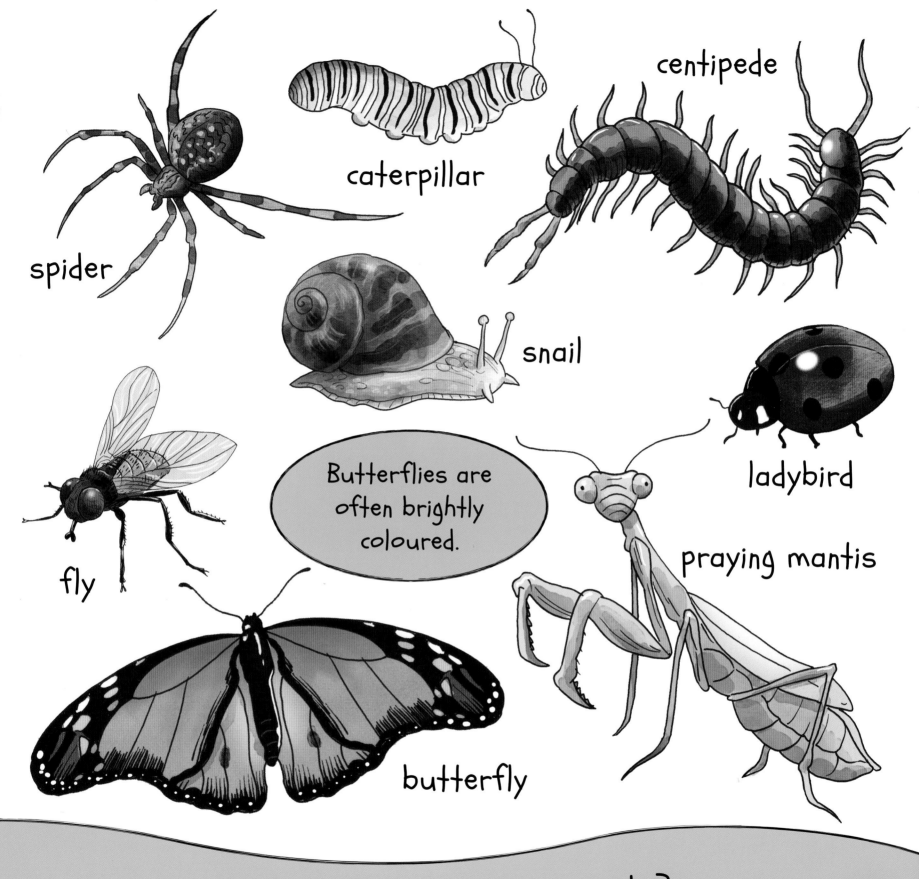

spider

caterpillar

centipede

snail

ladybird

fly

Butterflies are often brightly coloured.

praying mantis

butterfly

Pets

goldfish

pony

guinea pig

Dogs belong to the same family of animals as wolves.

chinchilla

dog

Which of these pets is a reptile?

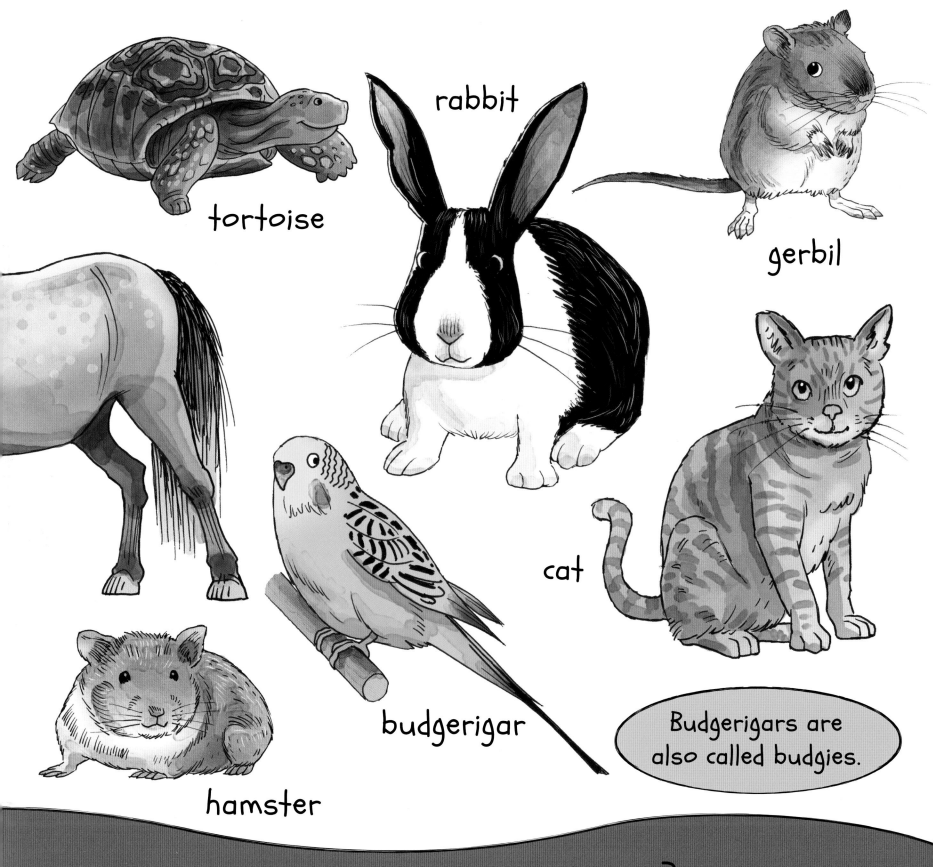

tortoise

rabbit

gerbil

cat

budgerigar

hamster

Budgerigars are
also called budgies.

Which of these pets do you have?

95

Can you find?

Look back on pages 74–95 to see if you can find the following animals.

giant panda

tree frog

crab

octopus

hippopotamus

duck

grasshopper

goldfish